Inside Machines
Trucks

David West

WINDMILL
BOOKS ™

Published in 2018 by **Windmill Books**,
an imprint of Rosen Publishing
29 East 21st Street, New York, NY 10010

Designed and illustrated David West

Cataloging-in-Publication Data
Names: West, David.
Title: Trucks / David West.
Description: New York : Windmill Books, 2018. | Series: Inside machines | Includes index.
Identifiers: ISBN 9781499483338 (pbk.) | ISBN 9781499483277 (library bound) | ISBN 9781499483154 (6 pack)
Subjects: LCSH: Trucks–Juvenile literature.
Classification: LCC TL230.15 W47 2018 | DDC 629.225–dc23

Manufactured in the United States of America

CPSIA Compliance Information: Batch BS17WM: For Further Information contact Rosen Publishing, New York, New York at 1-800-237-9932

Contents

Cement mixer

This truck carries cement in a large drum to a building site. The drum rotates to stop the cement from setting. At the building site, the driver reverses the rotation of the drum. The cement pours out down chutes to where it is needed.

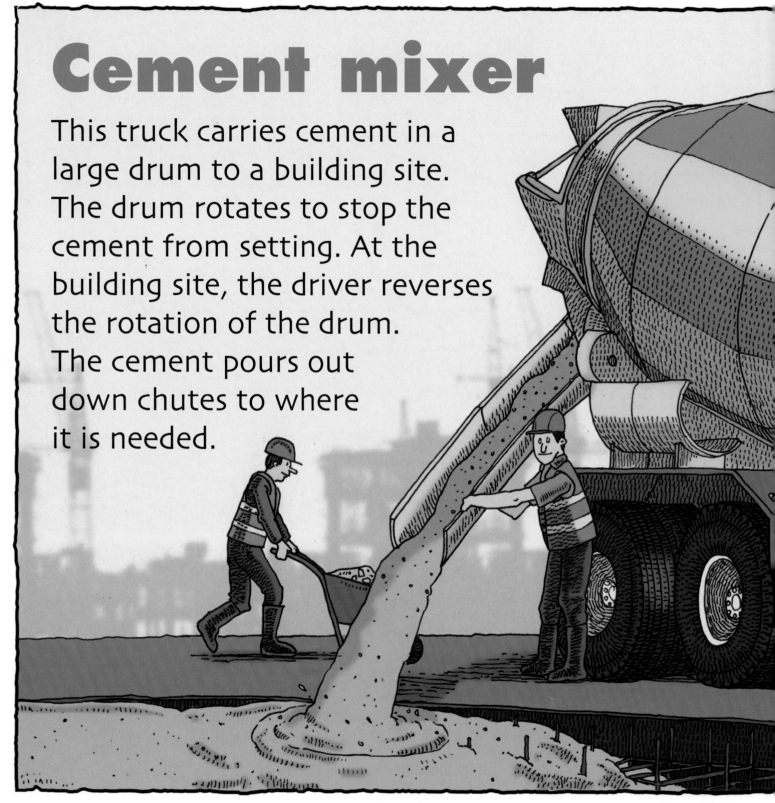

When the drum is empty, water is poured into it from the water tank. This washes away any bits of cement left in the drum.

Hopper
The cement mixture is poured into the drum through here.

Drum

Chutes
These can be joined together to carry the cement to where it is needed as it pours out of the drum.

Ladder

Spiral flights
This metal screw keeps the cement churning as the drum rotates. When the drum rotates the other way, the cement is forced out.

Cement mixture
This is made of sand, cement dust, and stones.

6

Inside a **Cement mixer**

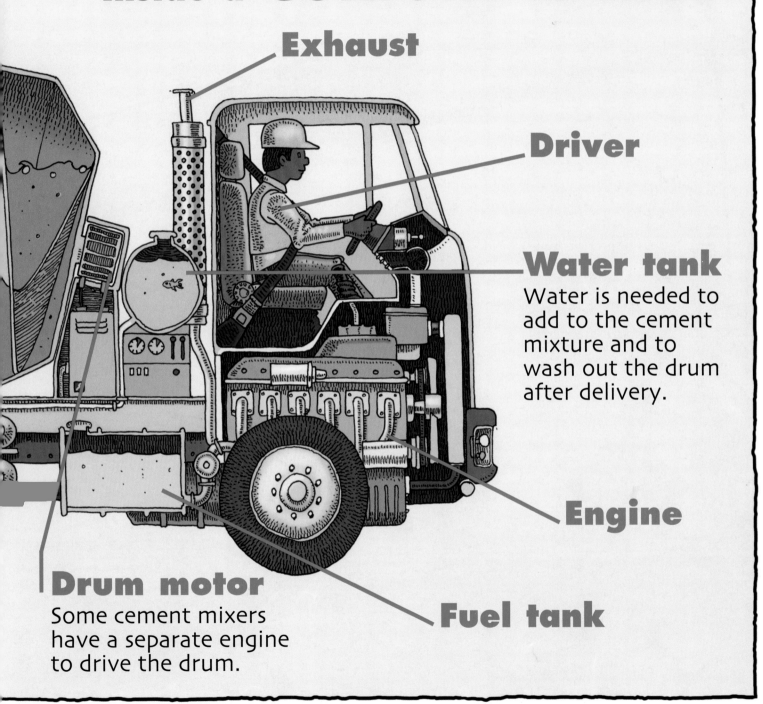

Exhaust

Driver

Water tank
Water is needed to add to the cement mixture and to wash out the drum after delivery.

Engine

Drum motor
Some cement mixers have a separate engine to drive the drum.

Fuel tank

Mobile cranes need to be very
stable when they lift heavy objects.
They have stabilizer legs which
extend out to keep the crane from
toppling over.

Mobile crane

This truck is designed to carry a crane. It has two engines. One drives the truck. The other operates the crane. The crane can be rotated all the way around to lift and drop things where they are needed. Its arm is called a boom. It extends out like a telescope to reach high or distant places.

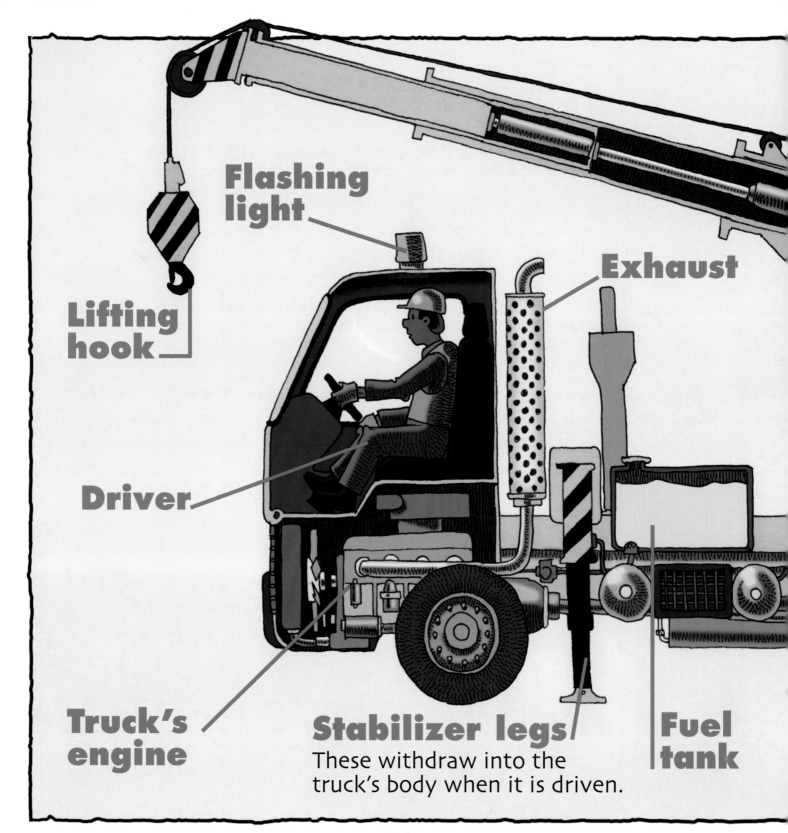

Flashing light

Exhaust

Lifting hook

Driver

Truck's engine

Stabilizer legs
These withdraw into the truck's body when it is driven.

Fuel tank

Inside a **Mobile crane**

Hydraulic ram

Telescopic boom

Hydraulic rams extend the crane's boom like a telescope.

Crane's engine

This engine operates the hydraulics that power the boom and the swinging gear.

Swinging gear

The swinging gear rotates the crane.

Up and down

This hydraulic ram moves the boom up and down.

Some garbage trucks, like this one, only collect recyclable materials such as paper, glass, and metal. Then it takes them to a recycling plant.

Garbage truck

These specially designed trucks carry garbage from our homes to landfill sites. Crews take bins full of garbage to the rear of the truck. Here they are picked up and emptied by the truck's hydraulics. Bags of garbage are thrown in and hydraulic rams push the garbage further back.

Inside a **Garbage truck**

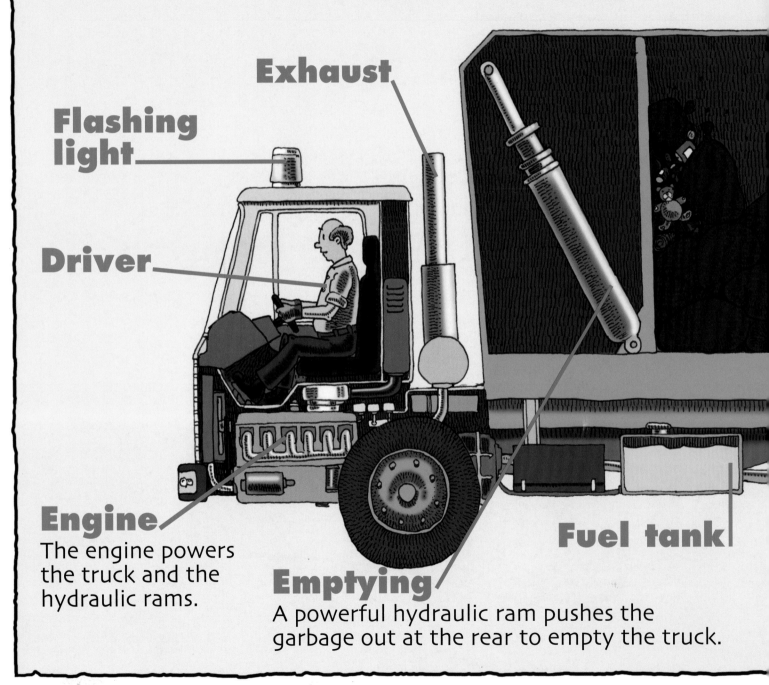

Exhaust

Flashing light

Driver

Engine
The engine powers the truck and the hydraulic rams.

Emptying
A powerful hydraulic ram pushes the garbage out at the rear to empty the truck.

Fuel tank

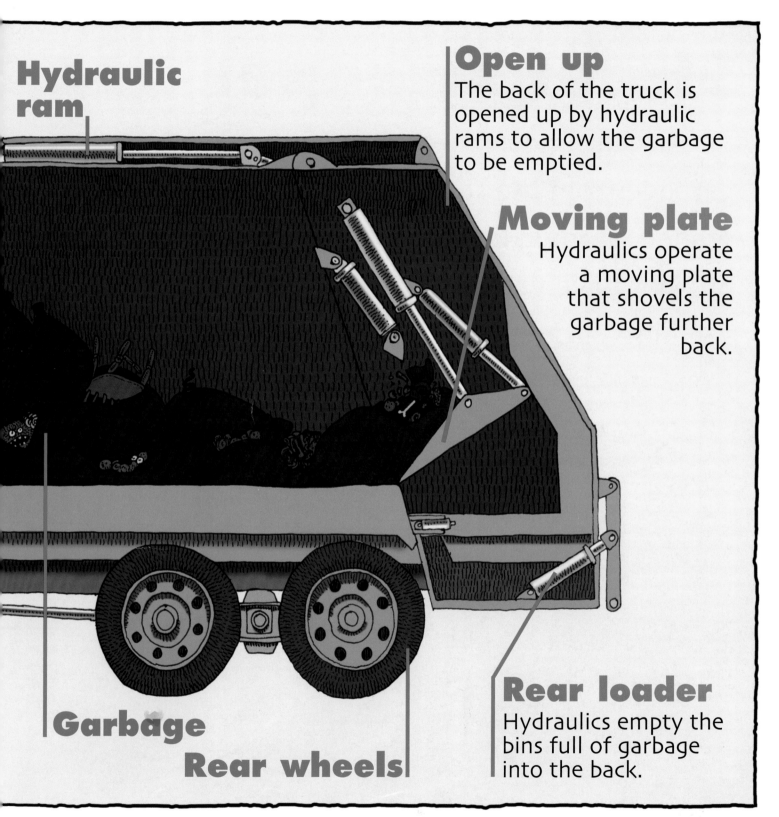

Hydraulic ram

Open up
The back of the truck is opened up by hydraulic rams to allow the garbage to be emptied.

Moving plate
Hydraulics operate a moving plate that shovels the garbage further back.

Garbage

Rear wheels

Rear loader
Hydraulics empty the bins full of garbage into the back.

Street sweeper

In cities around the world, small trucks clear garbage from the streets. They drive slowly with orange warning lights flashing. The circular brushes have **vacuums** behind them. The vacuums suck up leaves and garbage from the side of the road.

Street sweepers are often seen during the fall when piles of leaves need to be cleared away.

Inside a **Street sweeper**

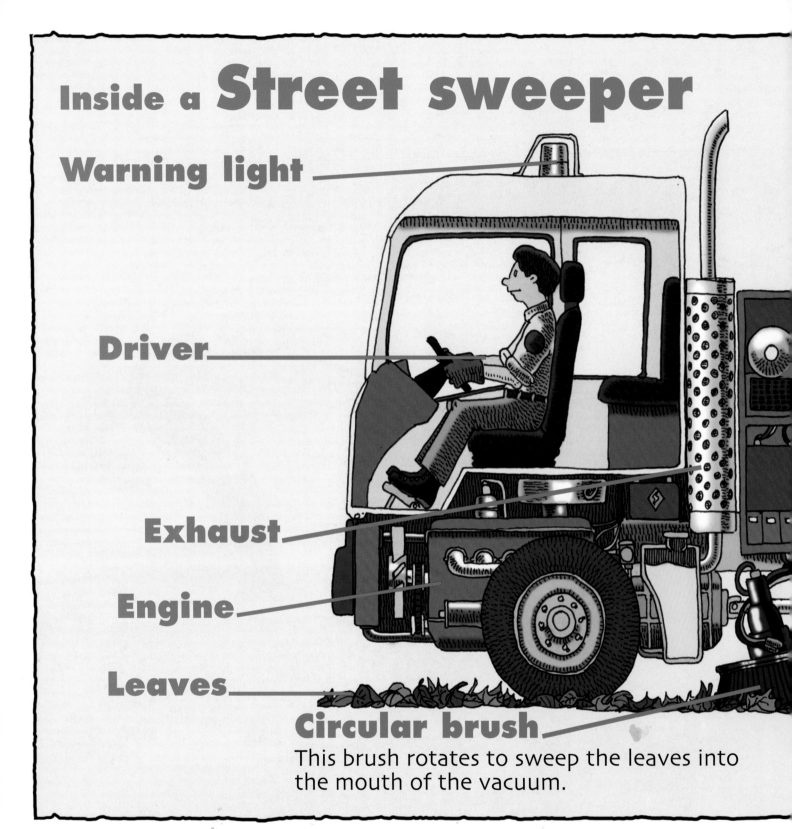

Warning light

Driver

Exhaust

Engine

Leaves

Circular brush
This brush rotates to sweep the leaves into the mouth of the vacuum.

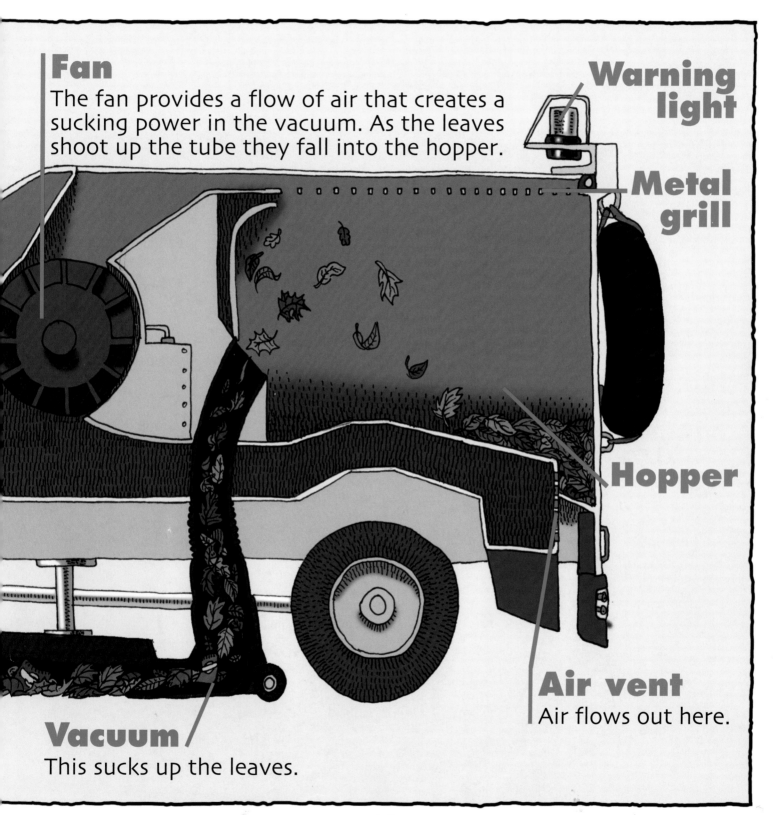

Fan

The fan provides a flow of air that creates a sucking power in the vacuum. As the leaves shoot up the tube they fall into the hopper.

Warning light

Metal grill

Hopper

Air vent

Air flows out here.

Vacuum

This sucks up the leaves.

Tow truck

These mighty machines are some of the most powerful trucks. Tow trucks are called out to tow away large vehicles, such as buses and trucks, that have broken down or been wrecked in a crash. They use their adjustable boom and **winch** to pull vehicles from ditches.

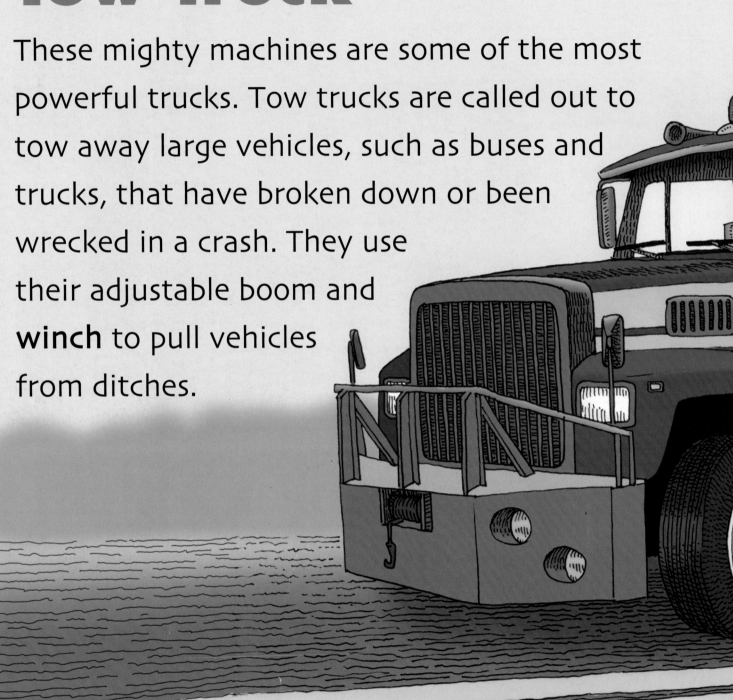

The biggest tow trucks can weigh up to 50 tons (45 metric tons). That's the same weight as six elephants!

Inside a **Tow truck**

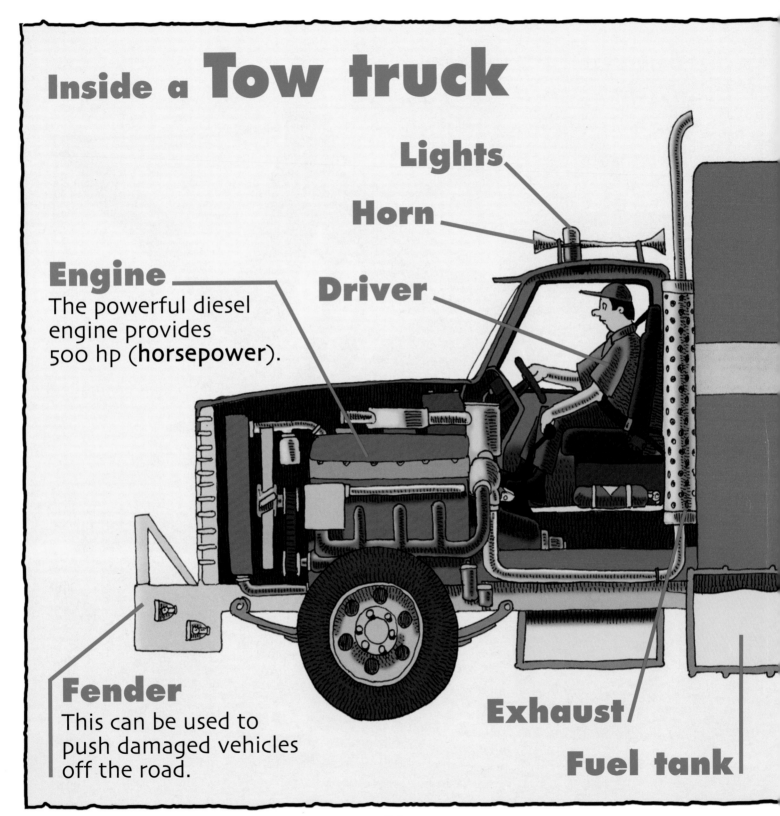

Lights

Horn

Engine
The powerful diesel engine provides 500 hp (**horsepower**).

Driver

Fender
This can be used to push damaged vehicles off the road.

Exhaust

Fuel tank

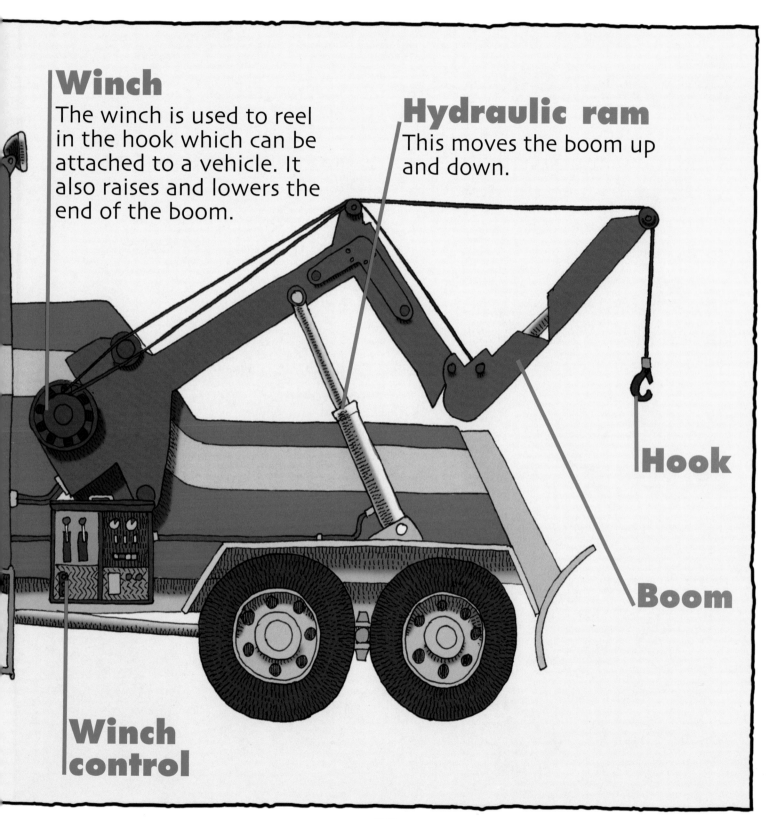

Winch

The winch is used to reel in the hook which can be attached to a vehicle. It also raises and lowers the end of the boom.

Hydraulic ram

This moves the boom up and down.

Hook

Boom

Winch control

Glossary

horsepower
A unit of measurement that is used to describe the power of engines.

hydraulic
The use of liquid to transfer power. Hydraulic rams use a special oil to move a piston up and down.

vacuum
A space with nothing in it (not even air). Also a device that sucks up material by using airflow to create a partial vacuum.

winch
A drum that is powered, has cable coiled around it, and is used to lift or haul heavy objects.

Index